Your Walk in Life

A Guide to Transforming
Your Pain into Peace

by
Alexa Servodidio, LCSW

CCB Publishing
British Columbia, Canada

Your Walk in Life: A Guide to Transforming Your Pain into Peace

Library and Archives Canada Cataloguing in Publication
Title: Your walk in life : a guide to transforming your pain into peace /
by Alexa Servodidio, LCSW.
Names: Servodidio, Alexa, 1973-, author
Description: First edition.
Identifiers: Canadiana (print) 2022017749X | Canadiana (ebook) 20220177511
| ISBN 9781771435079 (softcover) | ISBN 9781771435086 (PDF)
Subjects: LCSH: Anxiety—Popular works. | LCSH: Stress (Psychology)—Popular works.
| LCSH: Anxiety—Treatment—Popular works. | LCSH: Stress management—Popular works.
| LCSH: Mental health—Popular works.
Classification: LCC BF575.A6 S47 2022 | DDC 152.4/6—dc23

Front cover artwork: Footprints in the sand photo © Alexa Servodidio, LCSW

Back cover photo of Alexa Servodidio, LCSW by: Alison Sheehy
Website: https://www.alisonsheehyphotography.com
Facebook: https://www.facebook.com/alisonsheehyphotography
Instagram: https://www.instagram.com/alisonsheehyphoto
LinkedIn: https://www.linkedin.com/in/alisonsheehy/

Publisher: CCB Publishing
             British Columbia, Canada
             www.ccbpublishing.com

To Adeline

Contents

About Alexa Servodidio

Alexa Servodidio is more than just a therapist. She's a mom, a well-known TV and radio personality, and a relatable social media connection.

Her first book *Finding Your Peace Within the Chaos* quickly became a companion guide for surviving and thriving during the COVID pandemic. Her insight into navigating chaotic times has helped many to find balance over the last few years.

Nationally recognized for her syndicated television show, podcasts and speaking engagements, Alexa is always tuned-in to our connection with each other. Online she is known as 'Ask Alexa Therapy' across all social media platforms. Followers flock to her Facebook LIVE each Sunday to 'Ask Alexa' everything.

When she is not on-air, Alexa Servodidio is a Licensed Clinical Social Worker and Psychotherapist who has her own private practice. She works with individuals, couples, and families. Alexa has a Bachelor degree from Pace University and has a Master of Social Work degree from Fordham University.

Alexa's therapy practice in the shadow of New York City sees the new normal. People with hurdles and struggles to overcome. They are battling life; a life that can include ups and downs of all kinds: divorce, addictions, compulsions, destructive behaviors, and negative patterns. Imperfectly perfect people, like most of us. People who need someone to talk to, someone to trust. Alexa is that person. Not just because she's trained to be, because she simply is. It's her calling and she answered.

As we come out into the world again post-pandemic Alexa is planning a series of workshops focused on building community and connections. This new book is the center of that mission and a part of Alexa's walk in life. Please walk along with her, as you enjoy this book.

Find out more here:

https://www.askalexatherapy.com

Prologue

Learning to identify your walk in life is essential in finding your peace within the chaos. It may take many years of searching, researching, and discovering to be able to finally recognize your journey. Our walk is our own individual path. A path to establishing, defining, and maintaining a sense-of-self. Along this journey, there are various positive and negative external/internal factors we will experience. These experiences are stepping-stones which will become our foundations for empowerment. As we find ourselves at the many crossroads of life, take a moment to reflect and embrace your own process.

Chapter One

Nesting

Throughout my work in the mental health field I have learned that it is important to create a safe environment for my clients to explore themselves. I will identify the safe place as nesting. The term 'Nesting' can have numerous meanings, but for my practice it refers to the place created to allow individuals to become vulnerable and open.

In the chapters ahead I invite you, the reader, on this journey of hope, healing and growth. I will allow my readers to see through the eyes of the client and the clinician. You will have a bird's-eye view into the inner workings and steps that create "Your Walk In Life." As I say to my clients, "When looking for answers, struggling with pain, and researching ways to heal, be open to hear all and take what knowledge speaks to you." Start building your foundation and nesting place on these truths. These are your steps in life to developing and maintaining your sense-of-self.

Moving forward, I will be exploring and addressing the foundations for my practice. I will be introducing several case studies in order to illustrate various approaches that one can take. Know that you can incorporate more than one approach. Combining numerous methods can be life changing. I encourage each reader to be open and create a nonjudgmental space for themselves. Throughout this book these guidelines will be reinforced to remind the reader to keep them in the forefront of their mind. You will understand my reasoning as we go along.

I will be utilizing several case studies that are all unique, and each one has its own separate treatment plan.

The issues the clients are experiencing are wide-ranging and may not look similar. This is where I ask the reader to begin to ask themselves what issues could be reoccurring for these individuals.

Some examples of themes are not having a sense-of-self, not feeling good enough, feeling lost, feeling abandoned, and lacking self-worth. There are also many more that have not been mentioned. As you read through each chapter jot down themes you can identify, do not second-guess yourself. Then begin to explore your own walk in life to see if these themes are present.

At this point you might be feeling confused or overwhelmed, however don't worry because as we move along you will begin to understand my reasoning. Trust yourself and know that there is not a right or wrong way to do this. It is your right, it is your walk.

God Bless

Journaling Exercise #1

Write down any positive or negative themes/narratives that you are aware of that run through your mind on a daily basis.

_____

_____

_____

_____

_____

_____

_____

_____

_____

_____

_____

_____

_____

_____

_____

_____

_____

_____

_____

_____

_____

_____

_____
_____
_____
_____
_____
_____
_____
_____
_____
_____
_____
_____
_____
_____
_____
_____
_____
_____
_____
_____
_____
_____
_____
_____
_____

Chapter Two

EMDR Therapy

After a few years in private practice I began to hear more and more about EMDR (Eye Movement Desensitization and Reprocessing) Therapy. I was not familiar with it at all, and became very curious during a continuing education practicum. The continuing education course I was enrolled in had nothing to do with EMDR, but another colleague who was seated beside me had become my catalyst.

As the day progressed, we spoke about our backgrounds and practices. This clinician and I spoke about EMDR and her work surrounding it. She mentioned its many uses for all kinds of traumas, abuses, phobias and fears. I knew instantly I needed to learn more and began researching EMDR trainings and accredited clinicians. It didn't take long until I found Dr. Karen Alter Reid. She came highly recommended and I reached out to her immediately. Within a few months I began my 6-month trainings. At that point in time, I wasn't fully aware of how monumentally EMDR would impact myself as a clinician and my clients.

As noted above, EMDR stands for Eye Movement Desensitization and Reprocessing. This therapy utilizes bilateral eye movement to resource and reprocess memories, future events, goals, and stuck thoughts, to name a few. During the training we, the clinicians, became the client. We were asked to pick a traumatic memory and began reprocessing it.

Before a client begins reprocessing the clinician must first begin resourcing with the client in order to allow the client to access a sense of calmness. This resourced state could be a time when the client felt happy about themselves, an achievement, or place they've been to or not been to that they would consider their calm, safe place. When resourcing, the sets of bilateral eye movement range from 8 to 10 sets, and are slower in speed. This is necessary in order to reinforce the positive state for the client. An example of a safe, calm place could be the beach or could be the mountain tops. When the clinician feels comfortable that the client has found their calm place and are able to access it, and remain there, reprocessing can begin.

As we move forward with the next steps of EMDR, I will introduce a case study to illustrate the process.

Adam is a 65-year-old Hispanic, married male with a long history of incarceration, drug abuse (heroin), arrested for possession. As a child his father abandoned the family, and his mother raised four children alone. His mom has been described as providing the children with clothes, food and material things but was physically abusive when disciplining. The client has also been a victim of extreme trauma his whole life when he witnessed horrific accidents and abuse. The client is always paranoid and feels anxious that someone is trying to frame him. He reports feeling anxious all the time and has a very long history and tendency towards violence. The client has been out of prison for six years now which has been the longest time ever. The client feels he's being judged by his incarceration history. He says, "I keep everyone at an arm's length distance by being very loud and intimidating."

As we begin to formulate an EMDR protocol for this client there are a few necessary steps we need to explore with the client: a target memory, a negative cognition, a positive cognition, and a disturbance level. Once the target memory is identified, then the negative cognition can be explored. Then the touchstone can be identified. A touchstone memory is a memory that floats all the way back to childhood, the early years of life. This memory has been clouding the client's perceptions and thought process. The negative cognition is the negative statement the client feels about himself or herself. Examples of a negative cognition are: "I am alone," or "I am not safe," to name a few. Once the negative cognition is chosen we then pair with a positive cognition. I will have a list of both at the end of this chapter.

Before we pick Adam's negative cognition and pair it with what he feels is the positive cognition, we begin to explore Adam's safe/calm place. This is the place where he has been or would want to go. This is his happy place where he feels calm and safe. We want to make sure the calm place is a place that can't be tainted by any person, place, thing or negative memories. After we confirm the safe place, I will then begin to introduce the container. The container is a mental metaphor for a holding place for people, places, things and events that might come up during the reprocessing. The reason for the container is to empower the client to be able to lock unpleasant memories and thoughts that should arise into the container and put the container in your mind somewhere that is locked away. When a client and therapist agree that it's time to work on these memories the container will be opened mentally by the client. Some examples of a mental container can be a treasure chest, a ship, a safe, or even a toilet.

In the case study of Adam he has numerous traumatic memories. For this case let's conclude that the father abandoning the family was the touchstone memory. After exploring the negative cognition and positive cognition list with Adam let's say he chose the negative cognition of: I am alone. We would then ask the client to rate the memory 0 to 10, zero being not disturbing at all, and 10 the most disturbing. Thinking of that memory now, how disturbing is it for him? Let's say Adam rates it a 9. We then explore with the client what positive cognition feels right to him. "I am OK," is the positive cognition that best fits for him so he chooses it.

7

Now we begin the reprocessing. As a clinician, I will ask the client to bring up the memory and state the worst part of the memory. Once this has been completed I begin the reprocessing either by hand or using my light scan machine. This is when bilateral eye movement is utilized, and the sets will be longer in reprocessing than in resourcing. The sets will be 18 to 22 repetitions. When I refer to bilateral eye movement it is the left and right movement of your eyes while keeping your head still. This eye movement unblocks the stuck thoughts, feelings and body sensations/pains. By doing this the client is able to have a better lens into the trauma, pain, loss, or impulse. Oftentimes, many of my clients are seeing through the eyes of the traumatic event. By reprocessing the stuck thoughts and beliefs, the clinician and client are able to reprocess the traumatic events that have been blocking their journey to healing. This is where after each repetition, I will pause and ask the client to take a deep breath in and out and tell me if anything has come up.

What we are looking for are headlines. I will have instructed the client beforehand to imagine they are on the train moving very quickly looking out the window. This metaphor will describe the flashes of emotions, thoughts, body sensations and feelings that come along with reprocessing. I do not want the client to be stuck in one thought or feeling. Hence, I ask him to just identify the headlines. This is one of the other areas where EMDR differs from talk therapy. In EMDR, we don't have to go into every detail and explore every feeling. We can identify the main points and feelings and keep moving forward. After numerous repetitions and when the client reports the negative cognition has gone down to zero twice, I will ask the client to go back to the positive cognition. The client began with rating positive cognition 3, now the client rates it 7, which means he believes it is completely true. I then ask the client if he feels his body scan is clear and if there's any blockage. If the client reports clear, we have cleared this memory and I can move onto the next one. I have found that each client is unique and can differ in their response times.

Usually the first memory can be the hardest and take the longest to clear. As I remind my clients, this is not a race, we don't have to rush through this process. This is the time for the client to experience a sense of efficacy and empowerment. For more information about EMDR, please check out:

https://www.emdria.org

Remember: EMDR should only be conducted under the supervision of a licensed/trained professional. To find a more detailed list please search under negative and positive cognitions/EMDR. It is important to pair the negative and positive cognitions with the assistance of a trained EMDR clinician.

The following is a basic list: A clinician will guide you through finding the appropriate fit between negative and positive cognitions: NC/PC.

Example List of Positive and Negative Cognitions:

Negative Cognitions:

1) I am alone
2) I am helpless
3) I am worthless
4) I am not lovable
5) I am powerless
6) I am a bad person
7) I am a failure
8) The world isn't safe

Positive Cognitions:

1) I am enough
2) I am safe
3) I am worthy
4) I am powerful
5) I am trustworthy
6) I am successful
7) I am in control
8) I am capable

Journaling Exercise #2

Begin exploring possible negative cognitions that you have experienced, and then address how they have impacted your lens in life.

_____

_____

_____

_____

_____

_____

_____

_____

_____

_____

_____

_____

_____

_____

_____

_____

_____

_____

_____

Start exploring calm/safe places. While identifying calm places, tap into your 5 senses. Ask yourself these questions and provide as much detail as you can:

1) What do you hear?

_____

_____

_____

_____

_____

_____

_____

_____

_____

_____

_____

_____

_____

_____

_____

_____

_____

_____

2) What do you see?

_____

_____

_____

_____

_____

_____

_____

_____

_____

_____

_____

_____

_____

_____

_____

_____

_____

_____

_____

_____

_____

_____

3) What do you smell?

_____

_____

_____

_____

_____

_____

_____

_____

_____

_____

_____

_____

_____

_____

_____

_____

_____

_____

_____

_____

_____

4) What do you taste?

_____

_____

_____

_____

_____

_____

_____

_____

_____

_____

_____

_____

_____

_____

_____

_____

_____

_____

_____

_____

5) What do you feel?

_____

_____

_____

_____

_____

_____

_____

_____

_____

_____

_____

_____

_____

_____

_____

_____

_____

_____

_____

_____

_____

_____

Chapter Three

Your Walk in Life

Learning to identify your walk in life is essential to finding your peace within the chaos. It took many years of searching, and researching, and discovering before I was finally able to place a name on my journey. While in session with a client, the title "your walk in life" was coined. Throughout this book, I will explore the foundations for this practice.

Let's begin by defining what I mean when I say your walk in life. I will use the acronym YWIL moving forward to refer to your walk in life. YWIL begins before you are even aware of it. Each person's walk in life is unique. No two walks are the same; there may be similarities and common threads, but each walk is its own individualized path. This path is each individual's journey that will require them to define his or her sense-of-self. In life our sense-of-self can be affected by external and internal factors. These factors will possess positive and negative qualities that each individual will have to acknowledge, sit with, and process.

YWIL is grounded on this principle of how you react/respond to adverse and positive experiences. You have the power to adjust and adapt your thinking. I'm not saying that this is easy or fair, but unfortunately life isn't always fair. I'm not minimizing anyone's pain or suffering, but I firmly believe that healing begins with self-empowerment.

Through working with various clients, certain ideologies kept resurfacing. The first two I would like to explore are "untruths" and "truths." Let's begin with untruths. Untruths are beliefs held by a person based upon his or her own negative experiences which creates a false reality. This individual will believe in his or her untruths as if they were truths. Here are two examples:

Example #1:

This is a 32-year-old woman who grew up with a verbally abusive father and was told her whole life she was a disgrace and she didn't ever deserve to be happy. Her "untruth" is she believes that she's worthless, defective, and doesn't deserve to be loved. She bases her life perspective on this untruth as her truth.

Example #2:

This is a 50-year-old mother who has a long history of sexual abuse stemming from childhood by a trusted family friend. She was threatened often by her abuser never to tell anyone. Her untruth is: it was my fault, or why would I let something like this happen? As time goes by, these untruths evolve into various negative cognitions. This individual's negative cognition metamorphosed into: the world isn't safe, and no one is to be trusted. This untruth is manifested through her own children as she views the world as a dangerous place. The question then becomes how does one dismantle the untruths and identify the truth? This is where the need for a professional arises.

I am not saying a person can't process and heal on his or her own, but stated many times in EMDR, you went through the trauma alone, you don't have to go through the healing all by yourself. I found so many times in my practice that clients have kept these untruths to themselves due to guilt and shame. By exploring the trauma and releasing its silent hold on you, you can take your power back.

Through therapy a client can explore, define, and build his or her own sense-of-self foundation. This foundation will become the platform in which each person can use it as their truth. Through in-depth exploration and supportive therapy one can identify barriers and strengths. Many times a person can put his or her memories or flashbacks in a "bad box" so to speak. I refer to boxes and/or containers based on my EMDR training. A "bad box" is a place a person can put traumatic experiences, abuses, and losses. What makes this box so damaging is that if the person buries that box figuratively so far back in his or her mind that he or she will never be able to open it.

At first this can be viewed as a coping skill or defense mechanism. This is true in many cases of child sexual abuse where a child can't bear the burden emotionally, mentally and physically. However, as an adult if this child has never addressed this abuse, it could become a huge barrier to healing. The "good box" is referred to as the box you can put the same traumatic experiences in, but the difference is you have a trained professional to assist you. This box will not have control over when, where, or how you work through these experiences. The client becomes empowered by working with a therapist to be able to make decisions on where and when each memory will be addressed.

Why I believe this is so important to the healing process is because it allows the client to gain control over his or her own thoughts. This is a process that can take some time to achieve but through small victories, a client's confidence can be increased. The frequency and intensity of racing thoughts and paralyzing fears will be decreased. The client will begin to have a healthier lens to look through, and the edge of uncertainty will diminish.

Journaling Exercise #3

No judgment during this exercise.

1) Identify crossroads in your life.

_____

_____

_____

_____

_____

_____

_____

_____

_____

_____

_____

_____

_____

_____

_____

_____

_____

_____

_____

_____

_____

2) Write down your positive and negative reactions.

_____

_____

_____

_____

_____

_____

_____

_____

_____

_____

_____

_____

_____

_____

_____

_____

_____

_____

_____

_____

_____

_____

_____

_____

_____

_____

_____

_____

_____

_____

_____

_____

_____

_____

_____

_____

_____

_____

_____

_____

_____

_____

_____

_____

_____

_____

_____

_____

_____

Chapter Four

Positive Affirmations
and
Positive Thinking

As stated numerous times in my first book *Finding Your Peace Within the Chaos*, identifying your narrative is a key to unlocking stuck beliefs and thought patterns. What I mean by this is you need to become aware of how you speak to yourself. What is your monologue? Often there is a negative monologue that plays over and over again; sometimes we are not even aware of it. Observe your thoughts and how you perceive yourself and others. Also abstain from judgment and create your nesting space by allowing yourself to be vulnerable.

In order to illustrate this principle, let's read below our case study for Max.

Max is a 28-year-old male who reports feeling angry and anxious all the time. He works in fashion and has lost numerous jobs due to his anxiety. Max self-reports that when he becomes anxious, he begins to rage and act out on co-workers. In turn, he then feels ashamed. He also is concerned that he is not in a relationship at this time.

Let's begin to formulate possible negative monologues that might be running through Max's mind.

1. What is wrong with me? No one wants to be around me.

2. Everyone is laughing at me and my sad life.

3. I am a failure.

4. I'm scared, and I'm always going to be alone.

5. I am not good enough for my job and cannot find my significant other.

6. I will never be happy.

7 I am so angry all the time, and I'm out of control.

8. My anxiety controls me.

The next step is to start creating positive affirmations to match the negative statements. There is no right or wrong way to do this--it is what rings true for the individual that is important. The goal for the individual is to make a positive affirmation of his or her own so it can become part of their sense-of-self.

Some possible examples of positive affirmations can be:

1. Things are getting better.

2. I am okay.

3. I am good enough.

4. Rejection is God's protection.

5. I'm exactly where I'm supposed to be.

6. I have choices.

7. Every situation is an opportunity.

8. People want me to do well.

9. I will find happiness.

10. Let go and let God.

11. This too shall pass.

12. I'm working on myself.

By repeating a positive affirmation every time you catch yourself reciting the negative, will allow you to start retraining your thoughts/brain. Just like how you convinced yourself of all the negative thoughts, you will now allow the positive to be present.

It's okay if you do not believe them right away--it's fake it until you make it. In time your window of tolerance for the positive will increase as your negative will begin to decline. This does not happen overnight; give it time. This is a process. It cannot be forced or rushed. You are a work in progress--we are all works in progress. Remember to look at life as your walk and not as a competition. Remove the judgment and the negative monologues and replace them with a nesting place in whatever stage you are in. One cannot heal and grow while self-loathing and judgment are present.

Be open and embrace your positive and negative experiences as tools for self-reflection. Be patient and only utilize urgency as a positive tool. These lessons cannot be rushed. We must sit with them and be aware of where we are and observe them. Urgency is seen as a positive outlook of what there is to learn from and from what to allow yourself to explore. Heal and grow in God's timing. It is the best gift you can give yourself. Identify prior waiting periods in your life and then explore how you process waiting.

Journaling Exercise #4

1) Write down 10 positive affirmations.

1. _____

_____

2. _____

_____

3. _____

_____

4. _____

_____

5. _____

_____

6. _____

_____

7. _____

_____

8. _____

_____

9. _____

_____

10._____

_____

2) Recite these 10 positive affirmations daily.

3) Keep a journal of your mood and thoughts.

_____

_____

_____

_____

_____

_____

_____

_____

_____

_____

_____

_____

_____

_____

_____

_____

_____

_____

_____

_____

_____

_____

_____

_____

4) Rate your belief system and recite each positive affirmation
   for three months, record any changes.

_____

_____

_____

_____

_____

_____

_____

_____

_____

_____

_____

_____

_____

_____

_____

_____

_____

_____

_____

_____

_____

Chapter Five

Facing Challenges and Barriers

In life nothing is guaranteed, but anything is possible. Challenges and barriers pop up along our journey of finding and defining our sense-of-self. The key is to utilize these challenges as vessels for growth. It is easier said than done, but very achievable. Through each struggle, identify the lesson learned. When in the throes of it, it might be difficult, but beginning to gather all the pieces to this puzzle is key. When a person can dissect his or her challenges and barriers and break them down into separate components, this is when growth begins.

What is growth? Growth can be categorized into many different layers. The growth that I am focusing on is when my client can identify the challenge, acknowledge its impact on their quality of life, and then begin the healing process. The healing process doesn't mean at this point we have closure, peace, or even have begun a full exploration of the issue--rather, it represents the client's empowerment. By this I mean the client is able to become open to the process of healing. This is when it is possible to create a safe environment for the client to explore positive and negative experiences.

When a child grows up in an abusive, neglectful, or an addictive household, this safe environment does not exist. The chaos is a constant roller coaster of emotions that stunts the child's ability to safely explore and experiment. The child can become shut down. They are too frightened by their parents' erratic behaviors. And often when there is abuse, children learn that parents' emotions cannot be trusted. They begin to turn inward and blame themselves for their parents' behaviors.

During sessions, I collaborate with my clients in creating a safe environment. I become the vessel for the clients to practice, explore, and allow themselves to be that child they never could be in the past. Through this role modeling, clients can allow themselves to become vulnerable so they can start learning healthy childhood development.

I firmly believe that at any age a person can begin healing; they are gifted this experience of exploration. During this exploration, we will work collaboratively creating goals, outlines, and guidelines. The client will be able to explore different scenarios in his or her life without the negative cognition associated with it. The negative cognition will be identified, explored, dissected, and dismantled by working in tandem with the client. Doing this allows the client to begin empowerment. Empowerment becomes a basic human right to the client and not something they do not have access to. Utilizing positive affirmations as we discussed in the previous chapter will become the pillars to find the sense-of-self.

Now I will introduce the case study of Beatrice.

Beatrice is a 62-year-old divorced Caucasian woman with six children. The client self-reports history of being sexually abused by her father for many years as a child. The client became pregnant at one time with her father's child, which was sent to another country. The client reports being raped 5 years ago by a shopkeeper in her neighborhood. She reported the crime, but police stated, "He fled back to his country and there is nothing we can do." The client reports feeling anxious, angry, and sad. The client states that she is hyper-vigilant and browses chat rooms trying to entrap older perverted men who try to take advantage of young girls.

The case of Beatrice illustrates how as a child this client

was never able to feel safe. Beatrice learned at a young age that the people she is supposed to trust the most violated her trust. These are so many difficult layers for the clinician and client to work through; however, the establishment of the nesting place is key in order for any growth to occur. In this case, the idea of what a safe place is has to be introduced to the client for she most likely doesn't even know that one exists. So the question is then how do you facilitate this process with a client? I have found a method in my practice by utilizing role modeling, visualization, and trial and error.

This method facilitates the client's ability to access the meaning of safety. Also this empowers the client to be able to create her own safe place and build her sense-of-self. Often when there is abuse, trauma, and addiction, a feeling of hopelessness is present. A person can feel invisible and that she does not have any impact in this world. I encourage my clients to make their choices on their own, so moving forward the pillars for their sense-of-self-foundations are theirs and can't be taken away by any person or event. By doing this, I facilitate the client's ability to build and develop sense-of-self tools. I often refer to it as "the recipe."

The recipes are the various beliefs and experiences and thoughts that the client has gathered on her own to heal and grow. This is the positive recipe; however, there's also a negative recipe, but this should not be an anxiety provoking process. I work with the client to embrace the negative recipe as well. Sometimes in life we find out what we don't like first and what doesn't work for us before we identify what does. This is all part of your walk in life.

Journaling Exercise #5

1) Identify and define barriers/obstacles along with negative cognitions.

_____

_____

_____

_____

_____

_____

_____

_____

_____

_____

_____

_____

_____

_____

_____

_____

_____

_____

_____

_____

2) Explore their impact on your daily life.

3) Identify areas of growth.

_____

_____

_____

_____

_____

_____

_____

_____

_____

_____

_____

_____

_____

_____

_____

_____

_____

_____

_____

_____

_____

_____

Chapter Six

Where Do I Find My Sense-of-Self?

During each individual's stages of growth, identifying, building, and maintaining a sense-of-self is essential. As a therapist, I assist various clients in finding their sense-of-self. I have worked with clients at all stages of development and have found that an integral part of growth is having a strong sense-of-self. So many times we hear about knowing yourself, loving yourself, and self-care. These are the precedents that will shape and define your walk in life.

How you speak to yourself, treat yourself, and see yourself will teach the world how to treat you. In your journey of finding your sense-of-self, there will be ups and downs, road blocks and disappointments; however, you will learn that these are the exact opportunities for you to define who you are. How you sit with the uncomfortable feelings and wait for them to pass will build your confidence, your self-worth, and resilience.

Many times when exploring this journey with my clients, they can become overwhelmed and discouraged. It seems that this process will never end, but the good news is you will learn to embrace it. We don't have control over everything that happens in our lives, but we have control over how we decide to let go. What I mean by this is that we can decide to let go of trying to control every situation in our life. Let go of trying to control outcomes and how people react or respond. By doing this, we are releasing all of the stress we put on ourselves to make everything and everyone perfect. We can focus inward on ourselves and begin to trust ourselves. Strengthen your inner voice--begin trusting that no matter what life throws at you, you will survive and thrive. I'm not saying you won't ever be heartbroken, suffer loss or trauma again, but you will have the strength and wisdom that will allow you to make it through. This journey is a work in progress.

As I've said before, the goal isn't to master life, but instead to embrace it and embrace ourselves completely without judgment. Be able to look at yourself in the mirror and know you've done your best. Be proud of yourself and be able to acknowledge your accomplishments. Celebrate your growth. Reflect on your dark times and use them as evidence of strength. By doing this you are creating your sense-of-self on a daily basis. How you wait in life, develops your sense-of-self, builds your character and integrity. Maybe it will seem long and unbearable, but it is necessary in finding yourself. Even though relationships and dream jobs may not come to pass the way you envisioned, don't give up. Look for the lesson in the growth steps.

Here is the next case study of Mark and Melinda:

Mark and Melinda are high school sweethearts and have been married for 20 years. They have 3 children. Melinda reports Mark uses marijuana on a daily basis and is "high" all day and night. Mark self-reports drug use and states if he doesn't self-medicate then his anxiety and anger will escalate. Mark and Melinda report constant fighting.

Let's begin by identifying the growth steps and identify the barriers. Explore possible lessons one can learn. How would you begin building your sense-of-self as Mark? How do you begin building your sense-of-self as Melinda? What stages of development are each at currently? What are some positive coping skills each can utilize? What are some maladaptive ones? What are each one's goals? Make sure you remove any judgment. Allow yourself to step into Mark's shoes and then into Melinda's. What would you do? Don't worry--I'm not asking you to be a clinician, but you'll be creating a nesting place for yourself through this case study. Free yourself of any negative narratives and find your walk in life. I know you can do this.

Journaling Exercise #6

1) How do you describe yourself?

_____

_____

_____

_____

_____

_____

_____

_____

_____

_____

_____

_____

_____

_____

_____

_____

_____

_____

_____

_____

2) What are your strengths?

_____

_____

_____

_____

_____

_____

_____

_____

_____

_____

_____

_____

_____

_____

_____

_____

_____

_____

_____

_____

_____

_____

3) What area would you choose to work on for yourself?

_____

_____

_____

_____

_____

_____

_____

_____

_____

_____

_____

_____

_____

_____

_____

_____

_____

_____

_____

_____

_____

4) Are you able to objectively describe yourself without
   judgment?

_____

_____

_____

_____

_____

_____

_____

_____

_____

_____

_____

_____

_____

_____

_____

_____

_____

_____

_____

Chapter Seven

Adeline:
The Golden Thread

As I sit here about to write the last chapter, I'm wondering where to begin. As a therapist, it is protocol not to share personal information unless it will serve the client. In so many sessions with clients, I am asked, "How do I get through this?" "How do you know I can feel better?" "Why do you believe that I can do this?" Now I can share my answer--here is why.

As a therapist I speak with my clients about self-care, about never giving up, and that there's never a case that is too far gone. I believe in healing--physically, emotionally, mentally, and spiritually. It's not easy, and I don't know why we have to go through some horrific experiences in our lives. But I do know there's a light at the end of the tunnel. Sometimes we get there quickly, and sometimes it seems to last forever. However, never lose your hope.

As I sit here, almost 7 1/2 months pregnant now, I am feeling humbled as well as choked up to be sharing my story. Where to begin? My journey--to become pregnant-- was not an easy one, and I often suffered in silence. It was not anyone else's burden to bear, but it was my personal struggle to endure. This is when I say I practice what I preach comes into play. I can finally tell my story. I hope my story inspires, encourages and heals anyone reading this book. You're not alone.

For many years I've encountered questions concerning if I have children. For the most part, people were asking out of curiosity with a normal healthy intent; however, every time this question was asked, I felt the pain in my heart. I could never come back with an answer that I felt was good enough, so I always promised myself that one day I would divulge my secret pain in the hopes of teaching others to be careful of the questions you may ask. If someone wants you to know something, believe me, they will tell you.

A few years ago on November 4--I will never forget that date--I entered one of the darkest moments of my life. I just went through my dog Samson being diagnosed with bloat and having emergency surgery. I was told he probably would not make it, but it's a miracle he did. At the follow-up appointment, my vet notified me that Samson had a rare form of small cell lymphoma, really only found older cats; it hadn't been seen or treated before in any dogs and the prognosis was not good. I remember sitting at the animal hospital sobbing and feeling like I can't handle this. My dog just looked at me and tried to understand why I was so upset.

Samson began trying to console me, and I knew at this moment I had to somehow pull myself together and be strong for him. My mother taught me this valuable lesson many years ago when we found out that my dad had lung cancer. As I left the animal hospital I called my mom, my boyfriend at the time, and my spiritual mentor Rev. Garcia. We prayed, we cried, and I just sat in complete shock. I finally arrived home feeling like the world had stopped. Then my boyfriend came over so we could discuss things. He brought a box of tissues with him, stating that he had a feeling I might need them. Little did I know how much worse that day would become.

As time went by, he told me how we needed to talk. After a moment of silence, he told me he had come to a decision, and that he decided he changed his mind. He definitely did NOT want to have children. I was in shock and felt like I was kicked in the gut. I knew what I had to do. I ended the relationship. I knew I always wanted to have a child, and I would always resent him if I never tried.

After grieving the break-up for about nine months, I began my journey to become pregnant. The journey took me on a roller coaster, and at times, I felt discouraged. I prayed to God constantly asking for guidance and strength, and in August 2018, after five failed attempts, I heard the news I finally was waiting for--I was pregnant. I was so happy. I told my family and closest friends. Oh, I also told my ex-boyfriend who was genuinely happy for me.

I was in the beginning stages of my pregnancy not knowing what to expect when on August 28, after a few complications, I was told I had lost the baby. I felt like I couldn't breathe. I felt defeated. My doctor asked me what I wanted to do. How much do you have left in you? I told him I'm not giving up--I'm trying again! I began the process again in October 2019. I found out the procedure had not been completely successful, and I had another miscarriage. This miscarriage left me with extremely painful symptoms as well. I picked up my head and remembered what I tell my clients and began moving forward.

At this time I was still doing my radio show and television show, and one of my guests, medium Pamela Ellis, known as the Berkshire Medium, reached out to me about doing a reading. She had done previous readings for me during my radio shows, and it was incredible, so I agreed to do it. Pamela's readings are for people who have crossed over who come to speak to you through her. In this reading my dad had come through. Just as a side note, I have never met Pamela in person, only on Facebook, and she did not know me personally. Also no one except my mom, brother, and a few close friends knew of my pregnancy journey and recent miscarriages.

As the reading began, my dad and grandmother kept coming through when suddenly Pamela seemed a little confused or I would think disturbed. At one point she said, "Your dad is here. He's holding something. He has a message for you." She went on to say, "I don't know what this means, who's this is--but your dad is cradling a miscarried baby. He wants me to tell you he has your baby."

I began sobbing as we continued. My dad said to be strong and not to worry because I would have my baby. I would have my daughter. Pamela then inquired if I was interested in wanting to know if my last baby was a boy or a girl. I said, "Yes." She told me it was a girl. This is when I decided I needed to begin grieving the loss and not keep it a secret. I named my daughter Adeline and planted a small rosebush in her honor.

Unfortunately, miscarriages are very common, but rarely spoken about. I want to shed light on this loss and encourage my readers to open up. This tough dialogue is a loss no matter how far along you are--two weeks or six months--grieving is necessary in order to move on.

I would also like to add just one more thought going back to my previous point. Be aware of the questions you ask others. Days after I miscarried, I was asked by someone why I don't have any children. I wasn't strong enough at that time to go into my story, but I am now. Just be aware.

As my journey continues, I am humbled and so grateful that I am able to share my story with all of you. I know it has been a lot to handle and hard to hear, however I wanted to make sure all my clients, listeners, viewers, readers, friends, and family know this is why I know you can all do it. Don't give up. I know it's tough but as my dad would always say: This Too Shall Pass. God Bless and Amen.

Additional Journaling
Exercises for the Reader

Workbook Exercise #1

Children

1) Write down 5 statements about yourself that you think your parents don't know about you. It can be anything--nothing is too small.

1. _____

_____

_____

2. _____

_____

_____

3. _____

_____

_____

4. _____

_____

_____

5. _____

_____

_____

_____

2) Then write down 5 ways you can express how you feel about yourself to your parents.

1. _____

_____

_____

_____

2. _____

_____

_____

_____

3. _____

_____

_____

_____

4. _____

_____

_____

_____

5. _____

_____

_____

_____

_____

_____

3) What do you want them to hear?

_____

_____

_____

_____

_____

_____

_____

_____

_____

_____

_____

_____

_____

_____

_____

_____

_____

_____

_____

_____

_____

_____

Your Walk in Life

Workbook Exercise #2

Parents

1) Name 5 attributes that your child/children possess.

1. _____

_____

_____

2. _____

_____

_____

3. _____

_____

_____

4. _____

_____

_____

5. _____

_____

_____

_____

_____

_____

2) How have you expressed them to your child/children? List ways you have expressed them.

_____

_____

_____

_____

_____

_____

_____

_____

_____

_____

_____

_____

_____

_____

_____

_____

_____

_____

_____

_____

3) How would you know if they heard you? What is the evidence that they understood what you meant?

_____

_____

_____

_____

_____

_____

_____

_____

_____

_____

_____

_____

_____

_____

_____

_____

_____

_____

_____

4) How do you know that you have heard your child/children? What is the difference between your interpretation and what your child/children meant? Are there any differences? Are there any similarities?

_____

_____

_____

_____

_____

_____

_____

_____

_____

_____

_____

_____

_____

_____

_____

_____

_____

Workbook Exercise #3

Teenagers

1) Name 5 skills that you possess.

1. _____

_____

_____

2. _____

_____

_____

3. _____

_____

_____

4. _____

_____

_____

5. _____

_____

_____

_____

_____

_____

2) List when you have utilized them and how.

1. _____

_____

_____

_____

2. _____

_____

_____

_____

3. _____

_____

_____

_____

4. _____

_____

_____

_____

5. _____

_____

_____

_____

_____

Workbook Exercise #4

Parents and Teenagers

1) How do you know when your parents have heard what you are saying? Remember, there is a difference between hearing just the words and hearing the meaning.

_____

_____

_____

_____

_____

_____

_____

_____

_____

_____

_____

_____

_____

_____

_____

_____

_____

2) List signs that your parents have heard the meaning of what you are saying.

_____

_____

_____

_____

_____

_____

_____

_____

_____

_____

_____

_____

_____

_____

_____

_____

_____

_____

3) List the signs that you have heard what your parents are saying. Please provide any physical, verbal, or emotional indicators.

_____

_____

_____

_____

_____

_____

_____

_____

_____

_____

_____

_____

_____

_____

_____

_____

_____

_____

_____

_____

_____

Your Walk in Life

Workbook Exercise #5

Individual/Self

1) What is your window of acceptance for compliments?

_____

_____

_____

_____

_____

_____

_____

_____

_____

_____

_____

_____

_____

_____

_____

_____

_____

_____

_____

2) How do you feel when someone gives you positive feedback?

_____

_____

_____

_____

_____

_____

_____

_____

_____

_____

_____

_____

_____

_____

_____

_____

_____

_____

3) What is your window of tolerance for constructive feedback? How do you define the difference between constructive feedback and toxicity? What are your boundaries?

_____

_____

_____

_____

_____

_____

_____

_____

_____

_____

_____

_____

_____

_____

_____

_____

_____

_____

_____

_____

_____

_____

4) How do you teach others how to treat you?

_____

_____

_____

_____

_____

_____

_____

_____

_____

_____

_____

_____

_____

_____

_____

_____

_____

_____

_____

_____

_____

Workbook Exercise #6

Workplace/Employment

1) Name 3 strengths that you have pertaining towards your craft?

1. _____

_____

_____

_____

_____

2. _____

_____

_____

_____

_____

3. _____

_____

_____

_____

_____

2) Name 3 areas of difficulty.

1. _____

_____

_____

_____

_____

_____

2. _____

_____

_____

_____

_____

_____

3. _____

_____

_____

_____

_____

_____

3) What steps can you implement into your work routine each day to maintain balance?

_____

_____

_____

_____

_____

_____

_____

_____

_____

_____

_____

_____

_____

_____

_____

_____

_____

_____

_____

_____

_____

_____

Workbook Exercise #7

Family

1) Write down one positive word that describes each family member and explain why.

After completing the exercise, take that piece of paper, fold it, and place it in a jar. After each family member places their answers in a jar have each person pick one folded paper out of the jar and read each answer out loud. Then try and guess which family member it describes.

_____

_____

_____

_____

_____

_____

_____

_____

_____

_____

_____

_____

_____

_____

Workbook Exercise #8

Family Jar/Box Exercise

1) Place a jar or box in the kitchen. Write down on a small piece of paper every time a family member has done something that made you smile. Fold the piece of paper and place it back into the jar or box. At the end of the week tally up the votes. The family member with the highest number of times who made someone smile gets to pick what's for dinner that night.

Your Walk in Life

Workbook Exercise #9

Family Exercise

1) Place a closed box or an envelope that can be closed in an open area. Each family member will write down on a small piece of paper any time that they felt hurt by something another family member has said or done. At the end of the week, each family member will pick a piece of paper out of the box and read it.

This is to open up a discussion about the statement on the piece of paper. Remember, there's no judgment and make sure this is a safe, open environment for all family members to express themselves. Try to stay away from defending, blaming, shaming, or judging.

_____

_____

_____

_____

_____

_____

_____

_____

_____

_____

Workbook Exercise #10

Self-Empowerment

1) Write down every morning one task you would like to accomplish. Start with small and achievable goals.

Each night reflect on that task and the feelings surrounding the process.

_____

_____

_____

_____

_____

_____

_____

_____

_____

_____

_____

_____

_____

_____

_____

_____

_____